D0104298

THE
WISDOM
of
JUDAISM

THE
WISDOM
of
JUDAISM

Edited by
DALE SALWAK

Introduction by
RABBI YECHIEL ECKSTEIN

New World Library
Novato, California

New World Library
14 Pamaron Way
Novato, CA 94949

© 1997 Dale Salwak

Cover illustration and design by Cassandra Chu
Text layout and design by Aaron Kenedi

Library of Congress Cataloging-in-Publication Data

The wisdom of judaism / (edited by) Dale Salwak :
introduction by Yechiel Eckstein.

p.   cm
ISBN 1-57731-001-2 (cloth : alk. paper)
1. Judaism — Sacred books — Translation into English.
2. Judaism — Essence, genius, nature. 3. Ethics, Jewish.
I. Salwak, Dale.

BM495.W57 1997   97-5271
296.1 — dc21   CIP
                                                      r97

First printing, July 1997
Printed in the U.S.A on acid-free paper
ISBN 1-57731-001-2
Distributed to the trade by Publishers Group West

10 9 8 7 6 5 4 3 2

CONTENTS

PREFACE

Let those who are wise give heed to these things,
and consider the steadfast love of the Lord.

To do justice, to love goodness, to walk modestly
with God — these are among the highest ideals of
Judaism, ideals as important to us today as they were
to the prophet Micah who spoke them more than
2,500 years ago.

The heart of Judaism is a tradition of words
whose sources have been likened to an inverted pyra-
mid. At the base is the Bible — "the words of the
living God" — made up of the Law (the Torah or five
books of Moses), the Prophets (Nevi'im) and the
Writings (Ketuvim), all recorded over a period of
more than 1,300 years.

From this powerful base the tradition expands
outward to include the scholarly interpretations in
the Oral Torah or Talmud (comprising the Mishnah
and the Gemara) along with endless rabbinic stories

and legends (Midrash Rabbah), the legal codes, the mystical tradition (Zohar), and the book of organized prayer (Siddur), among others. Together, this vast body of literature has transformed the world and continues to guide and challenge millions of believers and nonbelievers alike.

While it would be impossible in a single book to include all of the words of wisdom expounded over nearly 6,000 years of diverse Jewish history, I have endeavored to compile and arrange thematically some of the most insightful and inspiring ethical and spiritual lessons, proverbs, maxims, and stories that answer these pressing questions of our day: Who is God? What is His will for our lives? What are His promises? What is the nature of good and evil? How can we live wisely?

At the core of Judaism is one central tenet: Human life is sacred, created in the image of God. We are given the free will to choose between good and evil. We are responsible and ultimately accountable for what we say and what we do, and there are rewards and consequences for moral behavior or misdeeds. We are our "brother's keeper," and we must be mindful of the suffering and needs of others as of our own. Indeed, in taking care of our fellow humans, we are caring for ourselves. "What is hateful to you," says the great Rabbi Hillel, "do not do to your neighbor."

In addition to the sanctity of life, these words describe God's laws. God made the world, He revealed His will to humanity, and He promised ultimate redemption to those who follow that will. He is universal and moral, an intensely personal God not only of judgment but of compassion, goodness, tenderness, care — and love. Fear God, trust Him, obey Him: That is the secret to living a balanced existence free from the self-deception, confusion, worry, or fear that can tear at the fabric of our lives and rob us of the joy, peace, and purpose that God has promised. These precepts are not abstractions but practical rules for everyday life, stemming ultimately from the commandments.

Further, the words of the Judaic tradition lead us to wisdom, which Aristotle called "the greatest good." Scripture tells us that wisdom is more precious than rubies, more important than longevity or riches or honor. The Book of Proverbs likens it to a "tree of life to those who lay hold of her"; and its author, Solomon, says that his writings are intended for acquiring "success, righteousness, justice, and equity," and also for "endowing the simple with shrewdness, the young with knowledge and foresight." Wisdom's "end and aim," says the Talmud, "is repentance and good deeds."

Thus the Judaic tradition commands us to live wisely — to see ourselves, others, and humanity's trials and triumphs from God's perspective. We are encouraged to acknowledge the great mystery in human life and to accept the innumerable challenges of growing up, of failure and folly, of achievement and hope, of joy and desire, endlessly changing from hour to hour through our allotted years from birth to death.

May the words that follow guide us in our quest for right action, speaking, and thinking, much as they have guided others before us to live the good and Godly life.

— DALE SALWAK

INTRODUCTION

For centuries, the predominant Christian view was that Jesus came to the world to bring mankind the possibility of salvation and eternal life. Without a belief in him, man could not reach the Father or be freed from the shackles of sin. What this viewpoint meant in terms of Judaism, which gave birth to Christianity, is that, with the dawn of the new Christian faith, Judaism ceased to be valid and was instead displaced by a triumphalist Christianity. Thus, in the new scheme of things, Christians became the new "people of God," the Hebrew Bible or Tanach became the "Old Testament," and Christianity became the exclusive *ortho δoxo* faith system through which one could achieve proper living and relationship with God.

Paul in Romans 9-11, on the other hand, seemed

to rail against such theological hubris and usurpation when he declared that God's promises to Israel are irrevocable. He warns Jesus' followers not to become haughty with their newfound spiritual possession, for the root supports the branch — not the branch the root. Tragically, Paul's warning was not heeded. For centuries, Christians adopted this "displacement theology," as it has come to be known, casting Judaism aside as though it died on the cross along with Jesus.

The situation today is not much better. While all Christian seminaries teach about Judaism in the Biblical period, those that teach about Jewish life after the first century are few and far between. Voltaire and the historian Toynbee reflected this triumphalist position best when they characterized Judaism as a relic, a "fossil religion," with no relevance or instructive purpose today.

What are the forces underlying such a condescending and arrogant theology? Are they oedipal in their origins? A rebellion against one's Jewish parentage? Are they part of an attempt to form one's own distinct identity by denying one's parents' legitimacy? Whatever their origin, this exclusivist theology led to the Marcian movement which, in the patristic period of the early Church, attempted to eliminate all vestiges of Christianity's Jewish roots —

including the Hebrew Bible (or to Christians, the Old Testament). Ultimately, the Church rejected Marcian's view, though not entirely. Indeed, it continued to belittle and degrade the Jewish faith along with the practitioners of that faith. They insisted there is no salvation outside the church, and there is no coming to the Father except through the son.

For centuries, Christianity effectively denied its Jewish roots and rejected its heritage, to their own detriment as well as to that of the Jewish people. The fact that Jesus was a Jew was buried under the rubble of polemic and fratricide. For centuries, Jews suffered oppression and persecution at the hands of those followers of Christ — and in his name — for the sin of rejecting the Christian faith. That this displacement theology which reduced the Jew and his faith to "pariah" status led to violence against Jews over the centuries is clear. What haunts us today is the realization that it may also have created the fertile groundwork and context in which the Holocaust was spawned.

In recent decades, there has been a dramatic change in the Church's relationship with the Jewish people and also with Christians' awareness of the Jewish roots of their own faith. Christians (and Jews, for that matter) are just beginning to come to grips with the fact that Jesus was a Jew and that they cannot be truly Christian without drawing sustenance from their Jewish roots. Put differently, Christians cannot begin to comprehend Jesus the Christ without first confronting Jesus the Jew of Nazareth.

This movement to recover Christians' roots in Judaism comes precisely at the time that the interfaith and ecumenical movements have become the important forces in American life that they have. We live in a pluralistic American society in which it is both inevitable and advantageous that we learn of one another — who the other truly is, not as we have come to stereotype them — and gain greater insight into one another's respective lives of faith.

The Wisdom of Judaism is a most welcome addition to this search for common ground between Christians and Jews and for greater understanding of the Jewish roots of the Christian faith. It brings to the fore the ancient wisdom of Judaism both before and after the rise of Christianity. And, while written originally first and foremost for Jews, these sources have a universal dimension and are instructive for all.

In this book, the reader will learn of the bankruptcy of commonly held stereotypes and caricatures that have perpetuated for centuries, many even to this very day. Hopefully, they will recognize that many of the facile theological dichotomies they may have grown up believing, such as that Christianity is the religion of love and Judaism the religion of law, the God of the "Old Testament" is the God of wrath while the God of the "New Testament" is the God of love, are precisely that — unfounded stereotypes, stemming from the historical polemic between two of God's faith communities.

The sources cited in this book are diverse — ranging from biblical quotes that carry with them the authority of the inerrant Word of God to those of the Midrash, that body of homiletic literature describing the beauty and love in Jewish tradition and ethics, to those rationalistic and legal writings of Maimonides in the 12th century. Hopefully, these texts shatter the notion that Jewish obedience to law is cold, sterile, unmerciful, and legalistic.

One of my favorite verses in the Tanach (Hebrew Bible) is "He has told you, O man, what is good, and what the Lord requires of you: only to do justice and to love goodness, and to walk modestly with your God" (Micah 6:8). *The Wisdom of Judaism* gives readers, Christians and Jews alike, the gift of Jewish wisdom over the centuries. More specifically, it teaches them how they can best fulfill Micah's concise dictum.

The Talmud tells the story of a Gentile who once came to Rabbi Shamai in the first century and asked him to explain all of Judaism while standing on one foot. Rabbi Shamai regarded him as imprudent and contemptuously threw him out of the house. When the gentile went to Rabbi Hillel, the wise Rabbi responded by paraphrasing the biblical verse, "Love thy neighbor as thyself" saying, "What is hurtful to you do not do unto others. Now go and study the rest."

Let this book be the beginning of our common search not only for wisdom but for how we might better uplift our souls and walk in the straight path, deepening our bonds of love with one another and strengthening our relationship with God and our devotion to Him.

Christians owe the Jewish people a debt of gratitude — for giving them their God, their Bible and the way to achieve salvation. In this book, the author shares another gift — the vision and wisdom of Judaism — with all who wish to partake. Now Christians as well as Jews can recover that dimension of holiness and Jewish spirituality described in our classical sources which had been buried and lost to Christians for centuries under the rubble of polemic. It is a gift we Jews gladly share with others — and hopefully study ourselves — so that we might all merit spiritual renewal and holiness in our lives.

Indeed, for Jews, there is no greater good deed and commandment than to study the Torah, God's blueprint of how we ought to lead our lives, in the here and now of this world. And so, let those who thirst for knowledge of the Lord and eagerly await the day when the "knowledge of the Lord will fill the earth like the waters in the sea" come and imbibe from the wisdom of Judaism.

— RABBI YECHIEL ECKSTEIN

CHAPTER ONE

The

NATURE

of

GOD

Creator

Do you not know?
Have you not heard?
The Lord is God from of old,
Creator of the earth from end to end....

— ISAIAH 40:28

He made the earth by His might,
Established the world by His wisdom,
And by His understanding stretched out the skies.

— JEREMIAH 10:12

You alone are the Lord. You made the heavens, the
highest heavens, and all their host, the earth and
everything upon it, the seas and everything in them.
You keep them all alive, and the host of heaven pros-
trate themselves before You.

— NEHEMIAH 9:6

The heavens declare the glory of God,
　　the sky proclaims His handiwork.

— PSALMS 19:1

When God began to create heaven and earth — the earth being unformed and void, with darkness over the surface of the deep and a wind from God sweeping over the water — God said, "Let there be light"; and there was light. God saw that the light was good, and God separated the light from the darkness. God called the light Day, and the darkness He called Night. And there was evening and there was morning, a first day....

The heaven and the earth were finished, and all their array. On the seventh day God finished the work that He had been doing, and He ceased on the seventh day from all the work that He had done. And God blessed the seventh day and declared it holy.... Such is the story of heaven and earth when they were created.

— GENESIS 1:1–5, 2:1–4

All that the Holy One created in the world He created in man.

— BABYLONIAN TALMUD, ABOT DE RABBI NATHAN 31

Beloved is man, for he was created in the image of God. But it was by a special love that it was made known to him that he was created in the image of God.

— MISHNAH, ABOT 3:18

When I behold Your heavens,
    the work of Your fingers,
    the moon and stars that You set in place,
    what is man that You have been mindful of him,
    mortal man that You have taken note of him,
    that You have made him little less than divine,
    and adorned him with glory and majesty;
    You have made him master over Your handiwork,
    laying the world at his feet. . . .

— PSALMS 8:4–7

It was You who created my conscience;
    You fashioned me in my mother's womb.
I praise You,
    for I am awesomely, wondrously made;
    Your work is wonderful;
    I know it very well.
My frame was not concealed from You
    when I was shaped in a hidden place,

knit together in the recesses of the earth.
Your eyes saw my unformed limbs;
    they were all recorded in Your book;
    in due time they were formed,
    to the very last one of them.

— PSALMS 139:13–16

Just as you do not know how the lifebreath passes into the limbs within the womb of the pregnant woman, so you cannot foresee the actions of God, who causes all things to happen.

— ECCLESIASTES 11:5

Who gives man speech? Who makes him dumb or deaf, seeing or blind? Is it not I, the Lord?

— EXODUS 4:11

The earth is the Lord's and all that it holds,
    the world and its inhabitants.

— PSALMS 24:1

Rich man and poor man meet;
The Lord made them both.

— PROVERBS 22:2

Of old You established the earth;
    the heavens are the work of Your hands.
They shall perish, but You shall endure;

they shall all wear out like a garment;
You change them like clothing
and they pass away.
But You are the same, and Your years never end.

— PSALMS 102:26–28

Let the nations not say,
"Where now is their God?"
when our God is in heaven
and all that He wills He accomplishes.

— PSALMS 115:2–3

Guardian and Guide

I turn my eyes to the mountains;
from where will my help come?
My help comes from the Lord,
maker of heaven and earth.

— PSALMS 121:1–2

While God's face is above, his heart is down below.

— Midrash, Song of Songs Rabbah 4, 4:9

In His hand is every living soul
And the breath of all mankind.

— JOB 12:10

God is peace, His name is peace, and all is bound
together in peace.

— ZOHAR, LEVITICUS 10B

The Lord bless you and protect you!
The Lord deal kindly and graciously with you!
The Lord bestow His favor upon you and grant you
      peace!

— NUMBERS 6:24–26

Safe and sound, I lie down and sleep,
      for You alone, O Lord, keep me secure.

— PSALMS 4:9

The confident mind You guard in safety,
In safety because it trusts in You.

Trust in the Lord for ever and ever,
For in Yah the Lord you have an everlasting Rock.

— ISAIAH 26:3–4

Though the misfortunes of the righteous be many,
      the Lord will save him from them all....

— PSALMS 34:20

The Lord is far from the wicked,
But He hears the prayer of the righteous.

— PROVERBS 15:29

A man to whom a calamity has occurred should make it known to the public, so that many people may entreat God's mercy for him.

— BABYLONIAN TALMUD, HULLIN 78A

To an earthly king, if a poor man greets him, or one who has a burn on his hand, it is a disgrace, and the king does not reply, but God is not so, everybody is acceptable to Him.

— MIDRASH, PSALMS RABBAH 147:1

The Lord is my light and my help;
    whom should I fear?

— PSALMS 27:1

In God, whose word I praise,
    in the Lord, whose word I praise,
    in God I trust;
    I am not afraid;
    what can man do to me?

— PSALMS 56:11–12

I am confident, unafraid;
For Yah the Lord is my strength and might,
And He has been my deliverance.

— ISAIAH 12:2

I adore you, O Lord, my strength,

O Lord, my crag, my fortress, my rescuer,

    my God, my rock in whom I seek refuge,

    my shield, my mighty champion, my haven.

— Psalms 18:2–3

God is our refuge and stronghold,

    a help in trouble, very near.

Therefore we are not afraid

    though the earth reels,

    though mountains topple into the sea —

    its waters rage and foam;

    in its swell mountains quake.

— Psalms 46:2–4

Trust in Him at all times, O people;

    pour out your hearts before Him;

    God is our refuge.

— Psalms 62:9

Gather the people to Me that I may let them hear My words, in order that they may learn to revere Me as long as they live on earth, and may so teach their children.

— Deuteronomy 4:10

The Lord is close to the brokenhearted;
    those crushed in spirit He delivers.

       — PSALMS 34:19

Because you took the Lord — my refuge,
    the Most High — as your haven,
    no harm will befall you,
    no disease touch your tent.
For He will order His angels
    to guard you wherever you go.
They will carry you in their hands
    lest you hurt your foot on a stone.
You will tread on cubs and vipers;
    you will trample lions and asps.

Because he is devoted to Me I will deliver him;
    I will keep him safe, for he knows My name.
When he calls on Me, I will answer him;
    I will be with him in distress;
    I will rescue him and make him honored;
    I will let him live to a ripe old age,
    and show him My salvation.

       — PSALMS 91:9–16

The way of God is perfect,

The word of the Lord is pure.
He is a shield to all who take refuge in Him.

— II SAMUEL 22:31

For I know that You are a compassionate and gracious God, slow to anger, abounding in kindness, renouncing punishment.

— JONAH 4:2

For as the heavens are high above the earth,
    so great is His steadfast love toward those who
        fear Him.
As east is far from west,
    so far has He removed our sins from us.

— PSALMS 103:11–12

He gives strength to the weary,
Fresh vigor to the spent.

— ISAIAH 40:29

I, I am He who comforts you!
What ails you that you fear
Man who must die,
Mortals who fare like grass?

— ISAIAH 51:12

Whom else have I in heaven?

And having You, I want no one on earth.

— PSALMS 73:25

Those who know Your name trust You,
    for You do not abandon those who turn to You,
        O Lord.

— PSALMS 9:11

A man may plot out his course,
But it is the Lord who directs his steps.

— PROVERBS 16:9

Examine me, O God, and know my mind;
    probe me and know my thoughts.
See if I have vexatious ways,
    and guide me in ways everlasting.

— PSALMS 139:23–24

O Lord, You have examined me and know me.
When I sit down or stand up You know it;
    You discern my thoughts from afar.
You observe my walking and reclining,
    and are familiar with all my ways.
There is not a word on my tongue
    but that You, O Lord, know it well.

— PSALMS 139:1–4

It is the way of a father to be compassionate and it is

the way of a mother to comfort. The Holy One said:
"I will act like a father and a mother."

— PESIKTA DE-RAB KAHANA 19:3

As a father has compassion for his children,
  so the Lord has compassion for those who fear
    Him.

— PSALMS 103:13

If one guards himself against sin three times, the Holy
One guards him from then on.

— JERUSALEM TALMUD, KIDDUSHIN 1:9

The Lord looks down from heaven;
  He sees all mankind.
From His dwelling-place He gazes
  on all the inhabitants of the earth —
  He who fashions the hearts of them all,
  who discerns all their doings.

— PSALMS 33:13–15

A woman once asked Rabbi Jose ben Halafta: "If cre-
ation was completed in only six days, what has God
been doing since?" He answered: "God spends His
time building ladders, for some to ascend, and others
to descend."

— MIDRASH, LEVITICUS RABBAH 8:1

I have heard your prayer, I have seen your tears.

— ISAIAH 38:5

Judge

Shall not the Judge of all the earth deal justly?

— GENESIS 18:25

For silver — the crucible;
For gold — the furnace,
And the Lord tests the mind.

— PROVERBS 17:3

Rabbi Akiva says, "Everything is foreseen, yet freedom of choice is given; the world is judged by grace, yet all is according to the preponderance of works."

— MISHNAH, ABOT 3:19

For not as man sees [does the Lord see]; man sees only what is visible, but the Lord sees into the heart.

— I SAMUEL 16:7

Think about three things and you will not be overcome by the desire to sin: Know what is above you; an eye that sees, an ear that hears, and all your actions are recorded in a book.

— MISHNAH, ABOT 2:1

Six things the Lord hates;
Seven are an abomination to Him:
A haughty bearing,
A lying tongue,
Hands that shed innocent blood,
A mind that hatches evil plots,
Feet quick to run to evil,
A false witness testifying lies,
And one who incites brothers to quarrel.

— PROVERBS 6:16–19

Thus says the Lord:
Cursed is he who trusts in man,
Who makes mere flesh his strength,
And turns his thoughts from the Lord.
He shall be like a bush in the desert,
Which does not sense the coming of good:
It is set in the scorched places of the wilderness,
In a barren land without inhabitant.

— JEREMIAH 17:5–6

Most devious is the heart;
It is perverse — who can fathom it?
I the Lord probe the heart,
Search the mind —

To repay every man according to his ways,
With the proper fruit of his deeds.

— JEREMIAH 17:9–10

As long as you execute the commandments, you are sanctified, but if you separate yourself from the commandments, you are profaned. And God says, "In this world the evil inclination [within every person's heart] separates you from the commandments, but in the world to come I will root it out from you...."

— MIDRASH, NUMBERS RABBAH 17:6

In the hour when an individual is brought before the heaven court for judgment, the person is asked:
    Did you conduct your [business] affairs
        honestly?
    Did you set aside regular time for Torah study?
    Did you work at having children?
    Did you look forward to the world's
        redemption?

— BABYLONIAN TALMUD, SHABBAT 31A

He who renders true judgments is a co-worker with God.

— MIDRASH, EXODUS RABBAH 18:13

The Lord! the Lord! a God compassionate and gracious, slow to anger, abounding in kindness and faithfulness, extending kindness to the thousandth generation, forgiving iniquity, transgression, and sin; yet He does not remit all punishment, but visits the iniquity of parents upon children and children's children, upon the third and fourth generations.

— EXODUS 34:6–7

As you did, so shall it be done to you;
Your conduct shall be requited.

— OBADIAH 1:15

There is no safety — said the Lord — for the wicked.

— ISAIAH 48:22

The Lord is a passionate, avenging God;
The Lord is vengeful and fierce in wrath.
The Lord takes vengeance on His enemies,
He rages against His foes....
Why will you plot against the Lord?
He wreaks utter destruction:
No adversary opposes Him twice!

— NAHUM 1:2, 9

Consider, all lives are Mine; the life of the father and

the life of the son are both Mine. The person who sins, only he shall die.

— EZEKIEL 18:4

Whoever can stop the members of his household from committing a sin, but does not, is held responsible for the sins of his household. If he can stop the people of his city from sinning, but does not, he is held responsible for the sins of the people of his city. If he can stop the whole world from sinning, and does not, he is held responsible for the sins of the whole world.

— BABYLONIAN TALMUD, SHABBAT 54B

They that are born are destined to die; and the dead to be brought to life again; and the living to be judged, to know, to make known, and to be made conscious that He is God, He the Maker, He the Creator, He the Discerner, He the Judge, He the Witness, He the Complainant; He it is that will in future judge, blessed be He, with whom there is no unrighteousness, nor forgetfulness, nor respect of persons, nor taking of bribes. Know also that everything is according to reckoning; and let not your imagination give you hope that the grave will be a place of refuge for you. For perforce you were formed, and perforce you were born, and perforce you live, and perforce you will die, and perforce you will in the future have to give account and reckoning before the King of kings, the Holy One, blessed be He.

— MISHNAH, ABOT 4:29

When man appears before the Throne of Judgment, the first question he is asked is not, "Have you believed in God," or "Have you prayed and performed ritual acts," but "Have you dealt honorably, faithfully in all your dealings with your fellowman?"

— BABYLONIAN TALMUD, SHABBAT 31A

The sum of the matter, when all is said and done: Revere God and observe His commandments! For this applies to all mankind: that God will call every creature to account for everything unknown, be it good or bad.

— ECCLESIASTES 12:13–14

CHAPTER TWO

GOD'S

COMMANDMENTS

Happy are those whose way is blameless,
who follow the teaching of the Lord.

— PSALMS 119:1

My son, heed my words;
And store up my commandments with you.
Keep my commandments and live,
My teaching, as the apple of your eye.
Bind them on your fingers;
Write them on the tablet of your mind.

— PROVERBS 7:1–3

You shall live by them [laws of the Torah], but you shall not die because of them.

— BABYLONIAN TALMUD, YOMA 85B

So follow the way of the good
And keep to the paths of the just.

— PROVERBS 2:20

You shall love the Lord your God with all your heart
and with all your soul and with all your might.

— DEUTERONOMY 6:5

You shall not hate your kinsfolk in your heart.
Reprove your kinsman but incur no guilt because of
him.

— LEVITICUS 19:17

A man should never impose an overpowering fear
upon his household.

— BABYLONIAN TALMUD, GITTIN 6B

He has told you, O man, what is good,
And what the Lord requires of you:
Only to do justice
And to love goodness,
And to walk modestly with your God. . . .

— MICAH 6:8

I the Lord am your God who brought you out of the
land of Egypt, the house of bondage: You shall have
no other gods besides Me.

— EXODUS 20:2–3

Turn to Me and gain success,
All the ends of earth!
For I am God, and there is none else.

— ISAIAH 45:22

You shall not make for yourself a sculptured image, or any likeness of what is in the heavens above, or on the earth below, or in the waters under the earth. You shall not bow down to them or serve them.

— EXODUS 20:4–5

You shall not swear falsely by the name of the Lord your God; for the Lord will not clear one who swears falsely by His name.

— EXODUS 20:7

You shall be holy, for I, the Lord your God, am holy.

— LEVITICUS 19:2

Remember the sabbath day and keep it holy. Six days you shall labor and do all your work, but the seventh day is a sabbath of the Lord your God: you shall not do any work.... For in six days the Lord made heaven and earth and sea, and all that is in them, and He rested on the seventh day; therefore the Lord blessed the sabbath day and hallowed it.

— EXODUS 20:8–11

The saving of life supersedes the Sabbath.

— BABYLONIAN TALMUD, SHABBAT 132A

Honor your father and your mother, that you may long endure on the land that the Lord your God is assigning to you.

— EXODUS 20:12

Parents shall not be put to death for children, nor children be put to death for parents: a person shall be put to death only for his own crime.

— DEUTERONOMY 24:16

You shall not murder.
You shall not commit adultery.

— EXODUS 20:13

If you are handsome, do not go astray after lewdness, but honor your Creator, and fear Him, and praise Him with the beauty which He has given you.

— MIDRASH, PESIKTA RABBATI 127A

You shall not steal.
You shall not bear false witness against your neighbor

— EXODUS 20:13

Do not deal basely with your countrymen. Do not profit by the blood of your fellow: I am the Lord.

— LEVITICUS 19:16

Teach your tongue to say, "I do not know," lest you be led to lie.

— BABYLONIAN TALMUD, BERAKHOT 4A

Do not be wise in your own eyes;
Fear the Lord and shun evil.

— PROVERBS 3:7

Keep far away from an evil neighbor, and don't become friendly with the wicked.

— MISHNAH, ABOT 1:7

You shall not wrong a stranger or oppress him, for you were strangers in the land of Egypt.

— EXODUS 22:20

If your enemy falls, do not exult;
If he trips, let your heart not rejoice,
Lest the Lord see it and be displeased,
And avert His wrath from him.

— PROVERBS 24:17–18

If your enemy is hungry, give him bread to eat;
If he is thirsty, give him water to drink.
You will be heaping live coals on his head,
And the Lord will reward you.

— PROVERBS 25:21–22

You shall not take vengeance or bear a grudge against your countrymen. Love your fellow as yourself: I am the Lord.

— LEVITICUS 19:18

For there will never cease to be needy ones in your land, which is why I command you: open your hand to the poor and needy kinsman in your land.

— DEUTERONOMY 15:11

You shall not covet your neighbor's house: you shall not covet your neighbor's wife, or his male or female slave, or his ox or his ass, or anything that is your neighbor's.

— EXODUS 20:14

Let your fellow man's property be as dear to you as your own.

— MISHNAH, ABOT 2:17

Be not like those who honor their gods in prosperity and curse them in adversity. In pleasure or pain, give thanks!

— MIDRASH, MEKILTA EXODUS 20:20

He who receives office in order to profit from it is like an adulterer, who gets his pleasure from a woman's body. God says, "I am called holy, you are called holy; if you have not all the qualities which I have, you should not accept leadership."

— MIDRASH, PESIKTA RABBATI 111A

As God is called merciful and gracious, so you be merciful and gracious, offering gifts gratis to all; as the Lord is called righteous and loving, so you be righteous and loving.

— MIDRASH, SIFRE DEUTERONOMY 85A

You shall rise before the aged and show deference to the old; you shall fear your God: I am the Lord.

— LEVITICUS 19:32

You shall have one standard for stranger and citizen alike: for I the Lord am your God.

— LEVITICUS 24:22

You shall not judge unfairly: you shall show no partiality; you shall not take bribes, for bribes blind the eyes of the discerning and upset the plea of the just.

— DEUTERONOMY 16:19

A philosopher asked Rabbi Reuven, "Who is the most hateful person in the world?"

"The person who denies his creator," Rabbi Reuven replied.

"Why is that?"

The rabbi answered: "Honor your father and mother; you shall not murder;...you shall not steal; you shall not bear false witness against your neighbor;...behold, a person does not repudiate any of these laws until he repudiates the root of them [God]."

— TOSEFTA, SHEBUOT 3:6

Talk no more with lofty pride,
Let no arrogance cross your lips!
For the Lord is an all-knowing God;
By Him actions are measured.

— I SAMUEL 2:3

But you must be very strong and resolute to observe faithfully all the Teaching that My servant Moses enjoined upon you. Do not deviate from it to the right or to the left, that you may be successful wherever you go. Let not this Book of the Teaching cease from your lips, but recite it day and night, so that you may observe faithfully all that is written in it. Only then will you prosper in your undertakings and only then will you be successful.

I charge you: Be strong and resolute; do not be terrified or dismayed, for the Lord your God is with you wherever you go.

— JOSHUA 1:7–9

Do not enter on the path of the wicked;
Do not walk on the way of evil men.

— PROVERBS 4:14

Thus said the Lord:
Let not the wise man glory in his wisdom;
Let not the strong man glory in his strength;
Let not the rich man glory in his riches.
But only in this should one glory:
In his earnest devotion to Me.
For I the Lord act with kindness,
Justice, and equity in the world;
For in these I delight
    — declares the Lord.

— JEREMIAH 9:22–23

Run to perform a light commandment as you would to perform the most important. Flee from sin, for one commandment leads to another commandment, and one sin brings about another.

— Mishnah, Abot 4:2

The words of Torah are compared to fire, for both were given from heaven, and both are eternal. If a man draws near the fire, he derives benefit; if he keeps afar, he is frozen, so with the words of the Torah: if a man toils in them, they are life to him; if he separates from them, they kill him.

— Midrash, Sifre Deuteronomy 143a

The biblical tales are only the Torah's outer garments, and woe to him who regards these as being the Torah itself!

— Zohar, Numbers 152a

God said, "Resemble Me; just as I repay good for evil so do you also repay good for evil."

— Midrash, Exodus Rabbah 26:2

Rabbi Simlai said, "Six hundred and thirteen commandments were given to Moses.... Then David came and reduced them to eleven [Psalm 15]. Then came Isaiah, and reduced them to six [Isaiah 33:15]. Then came Micah, and reduced them to three [Micah 6:8]. Then Isaiah came again, and reduced them to two, as it is said, 'Keep judgment and do righteousness.' Then came Amos, and reduced them to one, as it is said, 'Seek me and live.' Or one may say, then came Habakkuk [2:4], and reduced them to one, as it is said, 'The righteous shall live by his faith.'"

— BABYLONIAN TALMUD,
MAKKOT 23B–24A

O how I love Your teaching!
It is my study all day long.
Your commandments make me wiser than my
        enemies;
    they always stand by me.

— PSALMS 119:97–98

I arise at midnight to praise You
    for Your just rules.

— PSALMS 119:62

CHAPTER THREE

GOD'S

PROMISES

Blessed is he who trusts in the Lord,
Whose trust is the Lord alone.
He shall be like a tree planted by waters,
Sending forth its roots by a stream:
It does not sense the coming of heat,
Its leaves are ever fresh;
It has no care in a year of drought,
It does not cease to yield fruit.

— JEREMIAH 17:7–8

Many are the torments of the wicked,
    but he who trusts in the Lord
    shall be surrounded with favor.

— PSALMS 32:10

Do not envy a lawless man,

Or choose any of his ways;
For the devious man is an abomination to the Lord,
But He is intimate with the straightforward.

— PROVERBS 3:31–32

The wise shall obtain honor,
But dullards get disgrace as their portion.

— PROVERBS 3:35

As I [the Lord God] was with Moses, so I will be with
you; I will not fail you or forsake you.

— JOSHUA 1:5

No man bruises his finger here on earth unless it was
so decreed against him in Heaven.

— BABYLONIAN TALMUD, HULLIN 7B

The seal of God is truth.

— BABYLONIAN TALMUD, SHABBAT 55A

Grass withers, flowers fade —
But the word of our God is always fulfilled!

— ISAIAH 40:8

Now then, if you will obey Me faithfully and keep My
covenant, you shall be My treasured possession

among all the peoples. Indeed, all the earth is Mine, but you shall be to Me a kingdom of priests and a holy nation.

— EXODUS 19:5–6

If, then, you obey the commandments that I enjoin upon you this day, loving the Lord your God and serving Him with all your heart and soul, I will grant the rain for your land in season, the early rain and the late. You shall gather in your new grain and wine and oil — I will also provide grass in the fields for your cattle — and thus you shall eat your fill.

— DEUTERONOMY 11:13–15

Though my father and mother abandon me,
the Lord will take me in.

— PSALMS 27:10

The Lord makes poor and makes rich;
He casts down, He also lifts high.

— I SAMUEL 2:7

In the days to come,
The Mount of the Lord's House
Shall stand firm above the mountains
And tower above the hills;

And all the nations
Shall gaze on it with joy.

— ISAIAH 2:2; CF. MICAH 4:1

I [the Lord God] will pour out My spirit on all flesh;
Your sons and daughters shall prophesy;
Your old men shall dream dreams,
And your young men shall see visions.

— JOEL 3:1

For the Lord is good;
His steadfast love is eternal;
His faithfulness is for all generations.

— PSALMS 100:5

Man, his days are like those of grass;
he blooms like a flower of the field;
a wind passes by and it is no more,
its own place no longer knows it.
But the Lord's steadfast love is for all eternity
toward those who fear Him,
and His beneficence is for the children's children
of those who keep His covenant
and remember to observe His precepts.

— PSALMS 103:15–18

The Lord is gracious and compassionate,
    slow to anger and abounding in kindness.
The Lord is good to all,
    and His mercy is upon all His works.

— PSALMS 145:8–9

Many designs are in a man's mind,
But it is the Lord's plan that is accomplished.

— PROVERBS 19:21

Rend your hearts
Rather than your garments,
And turn back to the Lord your God.
For He is gracious and compassionate,
Slow to anger, abounding in kindness,
And renouncing punishment.

— JOEL 2:13

Rabbi Joshua ben Levi met Elijah at the mouth of the cave of Rabbi Simeon ben Yohai. He asked Elijah, "When will the Messiah come?" Elijah replied, "Go and ask him." "But where is he?" "At the gate of Rome." "And how shall I recognize him?" "He sits among the wretched who are suffering from sores; all the others uncover all their wounds, and then bind them all up again, but he uncovers and binds up each one separately, for he thinks, 'Lest I should be summoned and be detained.'"

Then Rabbi Joshua found him and said to him, "Peace be with you, my Master and Rabbi." The Messiah replied, "Peace be with you, son of Levi." He said, "When is the Master coming?" He replied, "Today."

Then Rabbi Joshua returned to Elijah, who said, "What did he say to you?" He replied, "Peace be with you, son of Levi." Elijah said, "Then he assured to you and your father a place in the world to come." The rabbi said, "He spoke falsely to me, for he said he would come today, and he has not come." Then Elijah said, "He meant 'today, if you hearken to His voice!' [Psalm 95:7]."

— BABYLONIAN TALMUD, SANHEDRIN 98A

Rabbi Baruqa of Huza often went to the marketplace at Lapet. One day, the prophet Elijah appeared to him there, and Rabbi Baruqa asked him, "Is there anyone among all these people who will have a share in the World to Come?" Elijah answered, "There is none." Later, two men came to the marketplace, and Elijah said to Rabbi Baruqa, "Those two will have a share in the World to Come!" Rabbi Baruqa asked the newcomers, "What is your occupation?" They replied, "We are clowns. When we see someone who is sad, we cheer him up. When we see two people quarreling, we try to make peace between them."

— BABYLONIAN TALMUD, TA'ANIT 22A

I call heaven and earth to witness: whether Jew or Gentile, whether man or woman, whether servant or freeman, they are all equal in this: that the Holy Spirit rests upon them in accordance with their deeds!

— MIDRASH, SEDER ELIYYAHU RABBAH 10

Even a Gentile, if he practices the Torah, is equal to the High Priest.

— MIDRASH, SIFRA 86B

He guards the steps of His faithful,
But the wicked perish in darkness —
For not by strength shall man prevail.

— I SAMUEL 2:9

Do not be sad, for your rejoicing in the Lord is the source of your strength.

— NEHEMIAH 8:10

Know that the Lord singles out the faithful for Him
    self;
    the Lord hears when I call to Him.

— PSALMS 4:4

The Lord is my shepherd;
 I lack nothing.
He makes me lie down in green pastures;
 He leads me to water in places of repose;
 He renews my life;
 He guides me in right paths
 as befits His name.
Though I walk through a valley of deepest darkness,
 I fear no harm, for You are with me;
 Your rod and Your staff — they comfort me.

You spread a table for me in full view of my enemies;
 You anoint my head with oil;
 my drink is abundant.
Only goodness and steadfast love shall pursue me
 all the days of my life,
 and I shall dwell in the house of the Lord
 for many long years.

      — PSALMS 23:1–6

Good and upright is the Lord;
 therefore He shows sinners the way.
He guides the lowly in the right path,
 and teaches the lowly His way.
All the Lord's paths are steadfast love

for those who keep the decrees of His covenant.

— PSALMS 25:8–10

Seek the favor of the Lord,
    and He will grant you the desires of your heart.
Leave all to the Lord;
    trust in Him; He will do it.

— PSALMS 37:4–5

Cast your burden on the Lord and He will sustain
    you;
He will never let the righteous man collapse.

— PSALMS 55:23

The righteous bloom like a date-palm;
    they thrive like a cedar in Lebanon;
    planted in the house of the Lord,
    they flourish in the courts of our God.
In old age they still produce fruit;
    they are full of sap and freshness,
    attesting that the Lord is upright,
    my rock, in whom there is no wrong.

— PSALMS 92:13–16

Your word is a lamp to my feet,
a light for my path.

— PSALMS 119:105

Be your sins like crimson,
They can turn snow-white;
Be they red as dyed wool,
They can become like fleece.

— ISAIAH 1:18

O you who love the Lord, hate evil!
He guards the lives of His loyal ones,
saving them from the hand of the wicked.
Light is sown for the righteous,
radiance for the upright.

— PSALMS 97:10–11

He will destroy death forever.
My Lord God will wipe the tears away
From all faces
And will put an end to the reproach of His people
Over all the earth —
For it is the Lord who has spoken.

— ISAIAH 25:8

Thus He will judge among the nations
And arbitrate for the many peoples,
And they shall beat their swords into plowshares
And their spears into pruning hooks:
Nation shall not take up
Sword against nation;
They shall never again know war.

— ISAIAH 2:4

Then man's haughtiness shall be humbled
And the pride of man brought low.
None but the Lord shall be
Exalted in that day.

— ISAIAH 2:17

...when My people, who bear My name, humble themselves, pray, and seek My favor and turn from their evil ways, I will hear in My heavenly abode and forgive their sins and heal their land.

— II CHRONICLES 7:14

I will heal their affliction,
Generously will I take them back in love;

For My anger has turned away from them.
I will be to Israel like dew;
He shall blossom like the lily,
He shall strike root like a Lebanon tree.

— HOSEA 14:5–6

For thus said He who high aloft
Forever dwells, whose name is holy:
I dwell on high, in holiness;
Yet with the contrite and the lowly in spirit —
Reviving the spirits of the lowly,
Reviving the hearts of the contrite.

— ISAIAH 57:15

The Lord is near to all who call Him,
 to all who call Him with sincerity.

— PSALMS 145:18

See, a time is coming — declares the Lord — when I
will make a new covenant with the House of Israel
and the House of Judah. It will not be like the
covenant I made with their fathers, when I took them
by the hand to lead them out of the land of Egypt, a
covenant which they broke, so that I rejected them —
declares the Lord. But such is the covenant I will

make with the House of Israel after these days —
declares the Lord: I will put My Teaching into their
inmost being and inscribe it upon their hearts. Then I
will be their God, and they shall be My people. No
longer will they need to teach one another and say to
one another, "Heed the Lord"; for all of them, from
the least of them to the greatest, shall heed Me —
declares the Lord.

For I will forgive their iniquities,
And remember their sins no more.

— JEREMIAH 31:31–34

Seek the Lord while He can be found,
Call to Him while He is near.
Let the wicked give up his ways,
The sinful man his plans;
Let him turn back to the Lord,
And He will pardon him;
To our God,
For He freely forgives.

For My plans are not your plans,
Nor are My ways your ways
        — declares the Lord.
But as the heavens are high above the earth,

So are My ways high above your ways
And My plans above your plans.

— ISAIAH 55:6–9

For as the rain or snow drops from heaven
And returns not there,
But soaks the earth
And makes it bring forth vegetation,
Yielding seed for sowing and bread for eating,
So is the word that issues from My mouth:
It does not come back to Me unfulfilled,
But performs what I purpose,
Achieves what I sent it to do.

— ISAIAH 55:10–11

In the World-to-Come, there will be no eating, or drinking, or procreation, or business, or jealousy or hatred or competition, but the righteous will sit with crowns on their heads feasting on the radiance of the shekhina, the divine presence.

— BABYLONIAN TALMUD, BERAKHOT 17A

I realized, too, that whatever God has brought to pass will recur evermore:

Nothing can be added to it
And nothing taken from it —

and God has brought to pass that men revere Him.

— ECCLESIASTES 3:14

All Israel have a portion in the World-to-Come.

— MISHNA, SANHEDRIN 11:1

I the Lord, in My grace, have summoned you,
And I have grasped you by the hand.
I created you, and appointed you
A covenant-people, a light of nations —
Opening eyes deprived of light,
Rescuing prisoners from confinement,
From the dungeon those who sit in darkness.

— ISAIAH 42:6–7

The righteous among the nations of the world will have a share in the World-to-Come.

— TOSEFTA, SANHEDRIN 13:2

No longer shall you need the sun
For light by day,
Nor the shining of the moon
For radiance;
For the Lord shall be your light everlasting,
Your God shall be your glory.

— ISAIAH 60:19

Trust in the Lord with all your heart,
And do not rely on your own understanding.
In all your ways acknowledge Him,
And He will make your paths smooth.

— PROVERBS 3:5–6

For the mountains may move
And the hills be shaken,
But my loyalty shall never move from you,
Nor My covenant of friendship be shaken
    — said the Lord, who takes you back in love.

— ISAIAH 54:10

The seal of God is truth.

— BABYLONIAN TALMUD, SHABBAT 55

CHAPTER FOUR

PRAISE BE

to

GOD

Let all that breathes praise the Lord.

— PSALMS 150:6

To do what pleases You, my God, is my desire;
　　Your teaching is in my inmost parts.

— PSALMS 40:9

Holy, holy, holy!
The Lord of Hosts!
His presence fills all the earth!

— ISAIAH 6:3

Raise a shout for God, all the earth;
　　sing the glory of His name;
　　make glorious His praise.

— PSALMS 66:2

It is good to praise the Lord,
> to sing hymns to Your name, O Most High,
> to proclaim Your steadfast love at daybreak,
> Your faithfulness each night. . . .

You have gladdened me by Your deeds, O Lord;
> I shout for joy at Your handiwork.

> — PSALMS 92:2–3, 5

Raise a shout for the Lord, all the earth;
> worship the Lord in gladness;
> come into His presence with shouts of joy.

> — PSALMS 100:1–2

This is the day that the Lord has made —
> let us exult and rejoice on it.

> — PSALMS 118:24

Praise the Lord, all you nations;
> extol Him, all you peoples,
> for great is His steadfast love toward us;
> the faithfulness of the Lord endures forever.
> Hallelujah.

> — PSALMS 117:1–2

O Lord, open my lips and my mouth shall speak your praises.

> — AMIDAH

I love the Lord
> for He hears my voice, my pleas;
> for He turns His ear to me
> whenever I call.

— PSALMS 116:1–2

Blessed art Thou, O Lord our God, King of the
> universe, who has created all things to his
> glory....

Blessed art Thou, O Lord, who makes bridegroom
> and bride to rejoice.

Blessed art Thou, O Lord, King of the universe, who
> created mirth and joy, bridegroom and bride,
> gladness, jubilation, dancing and delight, love
> and brotherhood, peace and fellowship

— BABYLONIAN TALMUD, KETUBOT 8A

The teaching of the Lord is perfect,
> renewing life;
> the decrees of the Lord are enduring,
> making the simple wise;

The precepts of the Lord are just,
> rejoicing the heart;
> the instruction of the Lord is lucid,
> making the eyes light up.

The fear of the Lord is pure,

abiding forever;
the judgments of the Lord are true,
righteous altogether,
more desirable than gold,
than much fine gold;
sweeter than honey,
than drippings of the comb.

— PSALMS 19:8–11

. . . Pour out your heart like water
In the presence of the Lord!

— LAMENTATIONS 2:19

O Lord, our Lord,
How majestic is Your name throughout the
earth. . . .

— PSALMS 8:2

Naked came I out of my mother's womb, and naked
shall I return there; the Lord has given, and the Lord
has taken away; blessed be the name of the Lord.

— JOB 1:21

You will teach me the path of life.
In Your presence is perfect joy;
delights are ever in Your right hand.

— PSALMS 16:11

Sing to the Lord a new song,
His praise from the ends of the earth....

— ISAIAH 42:10

Sing to the Lord a new song,
His praise from the ends of the earth....

— ISAIAH 42:10

CHAPTER FIVE

Our

RELATIONSHIP

with

GOD

Human Nature

O Lord, what is man that You should care about him,
  mortal man, that You should think of him?
Man is like a breath;
  his days are like a passing shadow.

— PSALMS 144:3–4

Rabbi Aha said, "God deliberated how to create man.
He said to himself, 'If I create him like the angels, he
will be immortal. If I create him like the beasts, he
will be mortal.' God decided to leave man's conduct to
his own free choice, and if he had not sinned, he
would have been immortal."

— MIDRASH, GENESIS RABBAH 8:11

There are three sins which no person avoids committing every day: sinful [lustful] thoughts, expecting

one's prayers to God to be answered immediately, and slander.

— BABYLONIAN TALMUD, BAVA BATHRA 164B

What is in your heart about your fellow man is most likely in his heart about you.

— SIFRE DEUTERONOMY, PISKA 24

A person's nature can be recognized through three things: his cup [drunkenness], his purse, and his anger.

— BABYLONIAN TALMUD, ERUBIN 65B

And the dust returns to the ground
As it was,
And the lifebreath returns to God
Who bestowed it.

— ECCLESIASTES 12:7

Just as the womb takes in and gives forth again, so the grave takes in and will give forth again.

— BABYLONIAN TALMUD, BERAKHOT 15B

Both [righteous and wicked] go to the same place; both came from dust and both return to dust.

— ECCLESIASTES 3:20

Who takes vengeance or bears a grudge acts like one who, having cut one hand while handling a knife, avenges himself by stabbing the other hand.

— JERUSALEM TALMUD, NEDARIM 9:4

Man makes a harness for his beast; all the more should he make one for the beast within himself, his evil desire.

— JERUSALEM TALMUD, SANHEDRIN 10:1

The body is the sheath of the soul.

— BABYLONIAN TALMUD, SANHEDRIN 108A

Just as God fills the whole world, so the soul fills the body. Just as God sees, but is not seen, so the soul sees, but is not itself seen. Just as God feeds the whole world, so the soul feeds the whole body. Just as God is pure, so the soul is pure. Just as God dwells in the innermost precincts [of the Temple], so also the soul dwells in the innermost part of the body.

— BABYLONIAN TALMUD, BERAKHOT 10A

People never leave this world with half their cravings satisfied. If they have a hundred, they want two hundred, and if they have two hundred, they want four hundred.

— MISHNAH, ECCLESIASTES RABBAH 3:12

A lover of money never has his fill of money, nor a lover of wealth his fill of income.

— ECCLESIASTES 5:9

... The eye never has enough of seeing,
Nor the ear enough of hearing.

— ECCLESIASTES 1:8

The heart alone knows its bitterness,
And no outsider can share in its joy.

— PROVERBS 14:10

More than all that you guard, guard your mind,
For it is the source of life.

— PROVERBS 4:23

The Holy Spirit rests on him only who has a joyous heart.

— JERUSALEM TALMUD, SUKKAT 5:1

An impatient man commits folly;
A man of intrigues will be hated.

— PROVERBS 14:17

A calm disposition gives bodily health;
Passion is rot to the bones.

— PROVERBS 14:30

He who commits adultery is devoid of sense;
Only one who would destroy himself does such a
    thing.

                        — PROVERBS 6:32

A joyful heart makes for good health;
Despondency dries up the bones.

                       — PROVERBS 17:22

A man's spirit can sustain him through illness;
But low spirits — who can bear them?

                       — PROVERBS 18:14

For man is born to [do] mischief,
Just as sparks fly upward.

                             — JOB 5:7

For there is not one good man on earth who does
what is best and doesn't err.

                      — ECCLESIASTES 7:20

Immorality in the house is like a worm in the vege-
tables.

               — BABYLONIAN TALMUD, SOTA 3B

The wicked man will be trapped in his iniquities;

He will be caught up in the ropes of his sin.

— PROVERBS 5:22

A man is allowed to follow the road he wishes to pursue.

— BABYLONIAN TALMUD, MAKKOT 10B

Who is strong? He who controls his passions.

— MISHNAH, ABOT 4:1

There are [always] thirty righteous men among the nations, by whose virtue the nations of the world continue to exist.

— BABYLONIAN TALMUD, HULLIN 92A

Repentance

Repentance makes man a new creature; hitherto dead through sin, he is fashioned afresh.

— MIDRASH, PSALMS RABBAH 18

A man cannot say to the Angel of Death, "Wait till I make up my accounts."

— MIDRASH, ECCLESIASTES RABBAH 8

Great is repentance; it turns premeditated sins into incentives for right conduct.

— BABYLONIAN TALMUD, YOMA 86B

The emptiest of you are as well-packed with religious observances as a pomegranate with seeds. For everyone who has the opportunity of committing a sin and escapes it and refrains from doing it performs a highly religious act. How much more, then, is this true of those "behind your veil," the modest and self-restrained among you!

— MIDRASH, CANTICLES RABBAH 4:4:3

Every human being may become righteous like Moses our Teacher, or wicked like Jeroboam; . . . merciful or cruel, miserly or generous, and so with all other qualities.

— MOSES MAIMONIDES,
MISHNAH TORAH, "LAWS OF REPENTANCE," 5:2

Rabbi Eliezer said, "Repent one day before your death."

His disciples asked him, "But does a person know on what day he [or she] is going to die?"

"All the more reason, therefore, to repent today,

lest one die tomorrow. In this manner, one's whole life will be spent in repentance."

— BABYLONIAN TALMUD, SHABBAT 153A

How is one proved to be a true penitent? Said Rabbi Judah: If the opportunity to commit the same sin presents itself on two occasions, and he does not yield to it.

— BABYLONIAN TALMUD, YOMA 86B

The end and aim of wisdom is repentance and good deeds.

— BABYLONIAN TALMUD, BERAKHOT 17

Rabbi Eliezer ben Jacob says, "He who carries out one good deed acquires one advocate in his own behalf, and he who commits one transgression acquires one accuser against himself. Repentance and good works are like a shield against calamity."

— MISHNAH, ABOT 4:13

Better is one hour of repentance and good works in this world than all the life of the World-to-Come, and better is one hour of calmness of spirit in the World-to-Come than all the life of this world.

— MISHNAH, ABOT 4:22

When the righteous man is in the town, he is its luster, its majesty, and its glory. When he leaves it, its luster, its majesty, and its glory depart.

— MIDRASH, GENESIS RABBAH 68:6

It is better for my enemy to see good in me than for me to see evil in him.

— YIDDISH PROVERB

Whoever saves one life, it is as if he saved the entire world.

— MISHNAH, SANHEDRIN 4:5

Happy is the man who makes the Lord his trust,
   who turns not to the arrogant or to followers of
   falsehood.

— PSALMS 40:5

The fear of the Lord is the beginning of knowledge;
Fools despise wisdom and discipline.

— PROVERBS 1:7

But let justice well up like water,
Righteousness like an unfailing stream.

— AMOS 5:24

As I live — declares the Lord God — it is not My desire that the wicked shall die, but that the wicked turn from his [evil] ways and live.

— EZEKIEL 33:11

Wash yourselves clean;
Put your evil doings
Away from My sight.
Cease to do evil;
Learn to do good.
Devote yourselves to justice;
Aid the wronged.

— ISAIAH 1:16–17

God is on the watch for the nations of the world to repent, so that He may bring them under His wings.

— MIDRASH, NUMBERS RABBAH 10:1

Sow righteousness for yourselves;
Reap the fruits of goodness;
Break for yourselves betimes fresh ground
Of seeking the Lord,
So that you may obtain a teacher of righteousness.

— HOSEA 10:12

Happy is he whose transgression is forgiven,
    whose sin is covered over.

— PSALMS 32:1

Prayer

Therefore let every faithful man pray to You....

— PSALMS 32:6

Rabbi Yohanan said, "Would that man could pray all day, for a prayer never loses its value."

— JERUSALEM TALMUD, BERAKHOT 1:1

Prayer should not be recited as if a man were reading a document.

— JERUSALEM TALMUD, BERAKHOT 4:3

Always let a man test himself: if he can direct his heart, let him pray; if he cannot, let him not pray.

— BABYLONIAN TALMUD, BERAKHOT 30B

The pious men of ancient times used to spend an hour [meditating], then pray, so that they could direct their heart towards their Father in Heaven.

— BABYLONIAN TALMUD, BERAKHOT 30B

Rabbi Elazar would first give a coin to a poor man, and then pray.

— BABYLONIAN TALMUD, BAVA BATHRA 10A

God longs to hear the prayer of the righteous.

— BABYLONIAN TALMUD, YEBAMOT 64A

...the prayer of the upright pleases Him.

— PROVERBS 15:8

...even an iron wall cannot separate God and Jew in prayer.

— BABYLONIAN TALMUD, PESAHIM 85B

Let not your prayer become a matter of routine, but let it be a plea for mercy and compassion.

— BABYLONIAN TALMUD, BERAKHOT 29B

A person is obligated to bless God for the evil that befalls him just as he blesses Him for the good.

— BABYLONIAN TALMUD, BERAKHOT 9:5

Prayer must mean putting one's very soul upon our hands, offering it to God.

— BABYLONIAN TALMUD, TA'ANIT 8A

Hear my voice, O Lord, at daybreak;
    at daybreak I plead before You, and wait.

— PSALMS 5:4

O Lord, God of my deliverance,
    when I cry out in the night before You,
    let my prayer reach You;
    incline Your ear to my cry.

— PSALMS 88:2–3

...all mankind comes to You,
You who hear prayer.

— PSALMS 65:3

As for the foreigners
Who attach themselves to the Lord,
To minister to Him.
And to love the name of the Lord,
To be His servants —
All who keep the sabbath and do not profane it,
And who hold fast to My covenant —
I will bring them to My sacred mount
And let them rejoice in My house of prayer....
For My House shall be called
A house of prayer for all peoples.

— ISAIAH 56:6–7

CHAPTER SIX

WISDOM

for

LIVING

Spoken Words

Keep your mouth from being rash, and let not your
throat be quick to bring forth speech before God. For
God is in heaven and you are on earth; that is why
your words should be few. Just as dreams come with
much brooding, so does foolish utterance come with
much speech. When you make a vow to God, do not
delay to fulfill it. For He has no pleasure in fools;
what you vow, fulfill. It is better not to vow at all than
to vow and not fulfill. Don't let your mouth bring you
into disfavor. . . .

— ECCLESIASTES 5:1–5

Where there is much talking, there is no lack of
    transgressing,
But he who curbs his tongue shows sense.

— PROVERBS 10:1

The Holy One hates him who says one thing in his mouth, and another in his heart.

— BABYLONIAN TALMUD, PESAHIM 113B

If there is anxiety in a man's mind let him quash it,
And turn it into joy with a good word.

— PROVERBS 12:25

Say little but do much.

— MISHNAH, ABOT 1:15

Just as one is commanded to say that which will be heeded, so is one commanded not to say that which will not be heeded.

— BABYLONIAN TALMUD, YEBAMOT 65B

A liar's punishment is that even when he tells the truth, he is not believed.

— BABYLONIAN TALMUD, SANHEDRIN 89B

A half-truth is a whole lie.

— YIDDISH PROVERB

Guard your tongue from evil,
    your lips from deceitful speech.

— PSALMS 34:14

Every dispute that is for a heavenly cause will ultimately endure.

— MISHNAH, ABOT 5:17

If two sit together and the words between them are of Torah, then the Shechinah [God's glory] is in their midst.

— MISHNAH, ABOT 3:2

Anger deprives a sage of his wisdom, a prophet of his vision.

— BABYLONIAN TALMUD, PESAHIM 66B

He who entreats aid for his comrade, though he himself is in need, is answered first.

— BABYLONIAN TALMUD, BABA KAMMA 92A

They who are insulted but do not insult, who hear themselves cursed and do not reply...the Bible says of them... "[They will be] like the sun as it rises in its might" (Judges 5:31).

— BABYLONIAN TALMUD, SHABBAT 88B

Instruct a wise man, and he will grow wiser;
Teach a righteous man, and he will gain in learning.

— PROVERBS 9:9

What the child says in the street is his father's words
or his mother's.

— BABYLONIAN TALMUD, SUKKAH 56B

Hatred stirs up strife,
But love covers up all faults.

— PROVERBS 10:12

A gentle response allays wrath;
A harsh word provokes anger.

— PROVERBS 15:1

Pleasant words are like a honeycomb,
Sweet to the palate and a cure for the body.

— PROVERBS 16:24

From all toil there is some gain,
But idle chatter is pure loss.

— PROVERBS 14:23

A shifty man stirs up strife,
And a querulous one alienates his friend.

— PROVERBS 16:28

Better a dry crust with peace
Than a house full of feasting with strife.

— PROVERBS 17:1

A rebuke works on an intelligent man
More than one hundred blows on a fool.

— PROVERBS 17:10

Even a fool, if he keeps silent, is deemed wise;
Intelligent, if he seals his lips.

— PROVERBS 17:28

Gold is plentiful, jewels abundant,
But wise speech is a precious object.

— PROVERBS 20:15

Bread gained by fraud may be tasty to a man,
But later his mouth will be filled with gravel.

— PROVERBS 20:17

For the lips of a forbidden [strange] woman
    drip honey;
Her mouth is smoother than oil;
But in the end she is as bitter as wormwood,
Sharp as a two-edged sword.

— PROVERBS 5:3–4

Who stops his ears at the cry of the wretched,
He too will call and not be answered.

— PROVERBS 21:13

Do not speak to a dullard,
For he will disdain your sensible words.

— PROVERBS 23:9

Do not be a witness against your fellow without good
    cause;
Would you mislead with your speech?

— PROVERBS 24:28

Like golden apples in silver showpieces
Is a phrase well turned.

— PROVERBS 25:11

Let the mouth of another praise you, not yours,
The lips of a stranger, not your own.

— PROVERBS 27:2

If you see a man hasty in speech,
There is more hope for a fool than for him.

— PROVERBS 29:20

These are the things you are to do: Speak the truth to
one another, render true and perfect justice in your
gates. And do not contrive evil against one another,
and do not love perjury, because all those are things
that I hate — declares the Lord.

— ZECHARIAH 8:16–17

May the words of my mouth
　　and the prayer of my heart
　　be acceptable to You,
　　O Lord, my rock and my redeemer.

— PSALMS 19:15

Marriage

The Lord God said, "It is not good for man to be alone; I will make a fitting helper for him."

— GENESIS 2:18

Hence a man leaves his father and mother and clings to his wife, so that they become one flesh.

— GENESIS 2:24

It was the custom that when a boy was born a cedar tree was planted and when a girl was born a pine tree. When they grew up and married, the wedding canopy was made of branches taken from both trees.

— BABYLONIAN TALMUD, GITTIN 57A

A man must always be exceedingly careful to show honor to his wife.

— BABYLONIAN TALMUD, BAVA MEZIA 59A

A man should love his wife as himself and honor her more than himself.

— BABYLONIAN TALMUD, YEBAMOT 62B

For love is fierce as death....
Vast floods cannot quench love,
Nor rivers drown it.

— SONG OF SONGS 8:6, 7

Rabbi Elazar said, "If a man divorces his first wife, even the altar sheds tears...."

— BABYLONIAN TALMUD, GITTIN 90B

He who loves his wife as himself; who honors her more than himself; who rears his children in the right path, and who marries them off at the proper time of their life, concerning him it is written: "And you will know that your home is at peace."

— BABYLONIAN TALMUD, YEBAMOT 62

A capable wife is a crown for her husband,
But an incompetent one is like rot in his bones.

— PROVERBS 12:4

Whoever marries a woman for her money will have disreputable children.

— BABYLONIAN TALMUD, KIDDUSHIN 70A

What a rare find is a capable wife!
Her worth is far beyond that of rubies.
Her husband puts his confidence in her,
And lacks no good thing.
She is good to him, never bad,
All the days of her life....

She is clothed with strength and splendor;
She looks to the future cheerfully.
Her mouth is full of wisdom,
Her tongue with kindly teaching.
She oversees the activities of her household
And never eats the bread of idleness.
Her children declare her happy;
Her husband praises her,
"Many women have done well,
But you surpass them all."
Grace is deceptive,
Beauty is illusory;
It is for her fear of the Lord
That a woman is to be praised.

— PROVERBS 31:10–12, 25–30

Children

God blessed them [male and female] and God said to

them, "Be fertile and increase...."

— GENESIS 1:28

When Rabbi Nahman and Rabbi Isaac were about to part, Rabbi Nahman asked Rabbi Isaac to bless him. Rabbi Isaac replied, "Let me tell you a parable. To what may this [having children] be compared? To a man who was traveling in the desert. He was hungry, tired and thirsty, when suddenly he came upon a tree whose fruits were sweet, its shade pleasant, and a stream of water was flowing beneath it. The man ate of the tree's fruits, drank of the water, and sat in the tree's shade. When he was about to continue his journey, he turned to the tree and said: 'Tree, O Tree, with what shall I bless you? Shall I say to you may your fruits be sweet? They are already sweet. That your shade be pleasant? It is already pleasant. That a stream of water flow by you? A stream of water already flows by you. Therefore, this is my blessing: May it be God's will that all the shoots planted from you be just like you.'"

"So it is with you," [Rabbi Isaac said to Rabbi Nahman]. "With what shall I bless you? Shall I wish you Torah learning? You already have learning. Wealth? You already have wealth. Children? You already have children.

"Therefore, this is my blessing: May it be God's will that your offspring will be like you."

— BABYLONIAN TALMUD, TA'ANIT 5B–6A

The love of parents goes to their children, but the love of these children goes to their children.

— BABYLONIAN TALMUD, SOTA 49A

When a father gives to his son, both laugh. When a son gives to his father, both cry.

— YIDDISH PROVERB

[Rabbi Meir taught:] When the Israelites came to the mountain of Sinai to receive God's word, the Torah, they discovered that God was not willing to give it without proof that they would cherish this precious gift. So God said to Israel: "Give Me guarantors that you will treasure My Torah." The people of Israel said: "Our ancestors will be our guarantors." God answered: "They are not sufficient. I have found fault with your ancestors. They would need guarantors for themselves!" The Israelites spoke again: "If You will not accept our ancestors, accept our Prophets — they will vouch for us." But God answered: "I have found fault with your prophets as well. They too would need their own guarantors. You may try one more time."

The Israelites, newly freed from the slavery of Egypt, looked up to the heavens and said to God: "If You will give us Your Torah, we will offer You our children." And God said: "Since you offer Me your children, I will give you My Torah."

— MIDRASH, SONG OF SONGS RABBAH 1:4

Your son is at five your master, at ten your servant, at fifteen your double, and after that, your friend or foe, depending on his bringing up.

— HASDAI IBN CRESCAS, C. 1230

Rabbi Judah says: Whoever does not teach his son a trade or profession teaches him to be a thief.

— BABYLONIAN TALMUD, KIDDUSHIN 29A

The best security for old age: respect your children.

— SHOLEM ASCH

One should not promise to give a child something and then not give it to him, because as a result, the child will learn to lie.

— BABYLONIAN TALMUD, SUKKAH 46B

Like mother, like daughter.

— EZEKIEL 16:44

A wise son brings joy to his father;
A dull son is his mother's sorrow.

— PROVERBS 10:1

He who lays in stores during the summer is a capable
son,
But he who sleeps during the harvest is an
incompetent.

— PROVERBS 10:5

Whoever brings up an orphan in his home is regarded
by the Bible as though the child had been born to
him.

— BABYLONIAN TALMUD, SANHEDRIN 19B

Train a lad in the way he ought to go;
He will not swerve from it even in old age.

— PROVERBS 22:6

Like arrows in the hand of a warrior
    are sons born to a man in his youth.

— PSALMS 127:4

Happy are the righteous! Not only do they acquire
merit, but they bestow merit upon their children and
children's children to the end of all generations. . . .

Woe unto the wicked! Not alone that they render themselves guilty, but they bestow guilt upon their children and children's children unto the end of all generations.

— BABYLONIAN TALMUD, YOMA 87A

There are three partners in man, God, father, and mother. When a man honors his father and mother, God says, "I regard it as though I had dwelt among them and they had honored me."

— BABYLONIAN TALMUD, KIDDUSHIN 30B

And all your children shall be disciples of the Lord,
And great shall be the happiness of your children. . . .

— ISAIAH 54:13

Do not reject the discipline of the Lord, my son;
Do not abhor His rebuke.
For whom the Lord loves, He rebukes,
As a father the son whom he favors.

— PROVERBS 3:11–12

Work

Great is labor; it confers honor on the laborer.

— BABYLONIAN TALMUD, NEDARIM 49B

If a man learns two paragraphs of the law in the morning and two in the evening and is engaged in his work all day, it is considered as though he had fulfilled the Torah in its entirety.

— TANHUMA BESHALLAKH #20

Scripture credits with performance not him who begins a task, but him who completes it.

— BABYLONIAN TALMUD, SOTA 13B

Lazybones, go to the ant;
Study its ways and learn.

— PROVERBS 6:6

Like vinegar to the teeth,
Like smoke to the eyes,
Is a lazy man to those who send him on a mission.

— PROVERBS 10:26

A lazy man craves, but has nothing;
The diligent shall feast on rich fare.

— PROVERBS 13:4

Through slothfulness the ceiling sags,
Through lazy hands the house caves in.

— ECCLESIASTES 10:18

Whatever it is in your power to do, do with all your might.

— ECCLESIASTES 9:10

Study

Take to heart these instructions with which I charge you this day. Impress them upon your children. Recite them when you stay at home and when you are away, when you lie down and when you get up. Bind them as a sign on your hand and let them serve as a symbol on your forehead; inscribe them on the doorposts of your house and on your gates.

— DEUTERONOMY 6:6–9

Turn it [Torah] over and over again, for one can find everything in it.

— MISHNAH, ABOT 5:22

Rabbi Tarfon and the other rabbis were once staying . . . in Lydda when the question was raised before them: "Is study greater or practice?" Rabbi Tarfon said, "Practice is greater." Rabbi Akiva said, "Study is greater." Then they all answered and said, "Study is greater for it leads to deeds."

— BABYLONIAN TALMUD, KIDDUSHIN 40B

One who learns from his companion a single chapter, a single law, a single verse, a single expression, or even a single letter, should accord him respect.

— MISHNAH, ABOT 6:3

Rabbi Akiva, illiterate at forty, saw one day a stone's perforation where water fell from a spring, and having heard people say, "Waters wear stones," he thought, "If soft water can bore through a rock, surely iron-clad Torah should, by sheer persistence, penetrate a tender mind"; and he turned to study.

— BABYLONIAN TALMUD, ABOT DE RABBI NATHAN 6

A foolish student will say, "Who can possibly learn the whole Torah ... ?" A wise student will say, "I will learn two laws today, and two tomorrow, until I have mastered the whole Torah."

— MIDRASH, SONG OF SONGS RABBAH 5:11

Every Jew is obligated to study Torah, whether he is poor or rich, in sound health or ailing, in the vigor of youth or very old and feeble.... Until what period in life ought one to study Torah? Until the day of one's death.

— MOSES MAIMONIDES, MISHNAH TORAH,
"LAWS OF TORAH STUDY," 1:8,10

Do not say, "When I have leisure, I will study." Perhaps you will have no leisure.

— MISHNAH, ABOT 2:4

Make your study of Torah a fixed, habitual activity.

— MISHNAH, ABOT 1:15

If you neglect the Torah, many causes for neglecting it will present themselves to you.

— MISHNAH, ABOT 4:12

As regards scholars, the older they become the more wisdom they acquire.... But as regards the ignorant, the older they become, the more foolish they become.

— BABYLONIAN TALMUD, SHABBAT 152A

Charity, Kindness, and Harmony

All men are responsible for one another.

— BABYLONIAN TALMUD, SANHEDRIN 27B

The whole world is sustained by God's charity; and the righteous are sustained by their own force.

— BABYLONIAN TALMUD, BERAKHOT 17B

Happy is he who is thoughtful of the wretched;
  in bad times may the Lord keep him from ha
                                    — PSALMS

If a person closes his eyes to avoid giving charity,
as if he committed adultery.
                — BABYLONIAN TALMUD, KETUBOT 6

The Jewish nation is distinguished by three charac
teristics; they are merciful, they are modest, and the
perform acts of loving-kindness.
              — BABYLONIAN TALMUD, YEBAMOT 79A

Jews are compassionate children of compassionate
parents, and one who shows no pity for fellow crea-
tures is assuredly not of the seed of Abraham, our
father.
              — BABYLONIAN TALMUD, BETZAH 32A

The world stands upon three things: upon the Law,
upon worship, and upon showing kindness.
                          — MISHNAH, ABOT 1:2

Shammai said: "Receive all people cheerfully."
                          — MISHNAH, ABOT 1:15

Speak up for the dumb,
For the rights of all the unfortunate.

— PROVERBS 31:8

Once, while Moses was tending the flock of his father-in-law, Jethro, one young sheep ran away. Moses ran after it until the sheep reached a shady place, where he found a pool of water and began to drink. When Moses reached the sheep, he said: "I did not know you ran away because you were thirsty. Now, you must be exhausted." Moses put the sheep on his shoulders and carried him. God said, "Because you tend the sheep belonging to human beings with such mercy, by your life I swear you shall be the shepherd of My sheep, Israel."

— MIDRASH, EXODUS RABBAH 2:2

Our rabbis have taught, We support the poor of the heathen along with the poor of Israel, visit the sick of the heathen along with the sick of Israel, and bury the [dead] poor of the heathen along with the dead of Israel, in the interests of peace.

— BABYLONIAN TALMUD, GITTIN 61A

He who is generous to the poor makes a loan to the
    Lord;

He will repay him his due.

— PROVERBS 19:17

One who gives charity in secret is greater than Moses.

— BABYLONIAN TALMUD, BAVA BATHRA 9B

Even a poor man who himself survives on charity should give charity.

— BABYLONIAN TALMUD, GITTIN 7B

Charity is equal in importance to all the other commandments combined.

— BABYLONIAN TALMUD, BAVA BATHRA 9A

A person is always liable for his actions, whether awake or asleep.

— BABYLONIAN TALMUD, BAVA KAMMA 3B

"Love your neighbor as yourself" (Leviticus 19:18) — this is the major principle of the Torah.

— PALESTINIAN TALMUD, NEDARIM 9:4

It happened that one of Rabbi Akiva's students became sick, but none of the sages went to visit him. Rabbi Akiva, however, went to visit him. Because he

111

swept and cleaned the floor for him, the student recovered. The student said to him, "Rabbi, you have given me life!" Rabbi Akiva came out and taught, "Those who do not visit a sick person might just as well have spilled his blood."

— BABYLONIAN TALMUD, NEDARIM 40A

Aid an enemy before you aid a friend, to subdue hatred.

— TOSEFTA, BABA METZIA 2:26

"Ye shall walk after the Lord your God" [Deuteronomy 13:4]. But how can a man walk after God who "is a devouring fire"? [Deuteronomy 4:24]. It means, walk after His attributes: clothe the naked, visit the sick, comfort the mourner, bury the dead.

— BABYLONIAN TALMUD, SOTA 14A

Greater is he who acts from love than he who acts from fear.

— BABYLONIAN TALMUD, SOTA 31A

Be not like servants who minister to their master upon the condition of receiving a reward; but be like servants who minister to their master without the condition of receiving a reward; and let the fear of

Heaven be upon you.

— MISHNAH, ABOT 1:3

Engage in Torah and charity even with an ulterior motive, for the habit of right doing will lead also to right motivation.

— BABYLONIAN TALMUD, PESAHIM 50B

One should choose to be among the persecuted, rather than the persecutors.

— BABYLONIAN TALMUD, BABA KAMMA 93A

Separate not yourself from the community.

— MISHNAH, ABOT 2:4

How good and how pleasant it is
    that brothers dwell together.

— PSALMS 133:1

Who is rich? One who is happy with what he has.

— MISHNAH, ABOT 4:1

Have we not all one father? Did not one God create us? Why do we break faith with one another, profaning the covenant of our fathers?

— MALACHI 2:10

Do not withhold good from one who deserves it
When you have the power to do it [for him].

— PROVERBS 3:27

Do not devise harm against your fellow
Who lives trustfully with you.

— PROVERBS 3:29

The whole of the Torah is for the purpose of promoting peace.

— BABYLONIAN TALMUD, GITTIN 59B

Humility

True sacrifice to God is a contrite spirit;
God, You will not despise
a contrite and crushed heart.

— PSALMS 51:19

The fear of the Lord is the discipline of wisdom;
Humility precedes honor.

— PROVERBS 15:33

Remember the days of old,
Consider the years of ages past;

Ask your father, he will inform you,
Your elders, they will tell you....

— DEUTERONOMY 32:7

The test of humility is your attitude to subordinates.

— ANONYMOUS, ORHOT TZADDIKIM, CHAPTER 2

As he came out of his mother's womb, so must he depart at last, naked as he came. He can take nothing of his wealth to carry with him.

— ECCLESIASTES 5:14

Man's life can be compared to a fox who found a vineyard, fenced in on all sides. There was one little hole in it, through which the fox wanted to get in. But it was too narrow, and he did not succeed. What did he do? He fasted for three days until he became thin and frail, and then entered through the hole. Once inside, the fox ate the grapes and grew fat. When he wanted to leave, however, he was again unable to fit through the hole. So once more he fasted for three days until he was thin and frail, and he went out.

Once outside, he turned towards the vineyard and said, "Vineyard, vineyard, how good is your fruit! All that is within you is beautiful and worthy of praise. But of what use are you? Just as one enters you, so one must come out."

So too with this world!

— MIDRASH, ECCLESIASTES RABBAH 5:14

A baby enters the world with hands clenched, as if to say, "The world is mine; I shall grab it." A man leaves with hands open, as if to say, "I can take nothing with me."

— MIDRASH, ECCLESIASTES RABBAH 5:14

First improve yourself, then improve others.

— BABYLONIAN TALMUD, BAVA MEZIA 107B

Torah abides only with him who regards himself as nothing.

— BABYLONIAN TALMUD, SOTA 21B

He who submits to the yoke of the Torah liberates himself from the yoke of circumstance. He rises above the pressures of the state and above the fluctuations of worldly fortune.

— MISHNAH, ABOT 3:6

Rabbi Yochanan ben Zakkai said: "Do not give yourself great airs if you have learned much Torah, because for this purpose you were created."

— MISHNAH, ABOT 2:8

Let all your deeds be done for the sake of Heaven.

— MISHNAH, ABOT 2:17

Be of an exceedingly humble spirit, for the end of man is the worm.

— MISHNAH, ABOT 4:4

Rabbi Me'ir said, "Whosoever labors in the Torah for its own sake merits many things; and not only so, but the whole world is indebted to him: he is called friend, beloved, a lover of the All-present, a lover of mankind; it clothes him in meekness and reverence; it fits him to become just, pious, upright, and faithful; it keeps him far from sin, and brings him near to virtue."

— MISHNAH, ABOT 6:1

No man is free, but he who labors in the Torah.

— MISHNAH, ABOT 6:2

So don't overdo goodness and don't act the wise man to excess, or you may be dumbfounded. Don't overdo wickedness and don't be a fool, or you may die before your time.

— ECCLESIASTES 7:16–17

Before ruin a man's heart is proud;
Humility goes before honor.

— PROVERBS 18:12

Repute is preferable to great wealth,
Grace is better than silver and gold.

— PROVERBS 22:1

A man's pride will humiliate him,
But a humble man will obtain honor.

— PROVERBS 29:23

Study of Torah leads to precision, precision to zeal,
zeal to cleanliness, cleanliness to restraint, restraint to
purity, purity to holiness, holiness to meekness,
meekness to fear of sin, fear of sin to saintliness, saintliness to the holy spirit, and the holy spirit to life eternal.

— BABYLONIAN TALMUD, ABODA ZARA 20B

Rabbi Yohanan ben Zakkai said, "Just as the sin-
offering atones for Israel, so righteousness atones for
the peoples of the world."

— BABYLONIAN TALMUD, BABA BATRA 10B

Lay no burden on the public which the majority

cannot bear.

— Babylonian Talmud, Baba Batra 60b

God weeps . . . over a leader who domineers over the community.

— Babylonian Talmud, Hagiga 5b

Do not judge thy comrade until thou hast stood in his place.

— Mishnah, Abot 2:5

The bows of the mighty are broken,
And the faltering are girded with strength.

— I Samuel 2:4

When arrogance appears, disgrace follows,
But wisdom is with those who are unassuming.

— Proverbs 11:2

Pride goes before ruin,
Arrogance, before failure.

— Proverbs 16:18

A season is set for everything, a time for every
     experience under heaven:
A time for being born and a time for dying,

A time for planting and a time for uprooting the
    planted;
A time for slaying and a time for healing,
A time for tearing down and a time for building up;
A time for weeping and a time for laughing,
A time for wailing and a time for dancing;
A time for throwing stones and a time for gathering
    stones,
A time for embracing and a time for shunning
    embraces;
A time for seeking and a time for losing,
A time for keeping and a time for discarding;
A time for ripping and a time for sewing,
A time for silence and a time for speaking;
A time for loving and a time for hating;
A time for war and a time for peace.

— ECCLESIASTES 3:1–8

Thus I realized that the only worthwhile thing there is
for them is to enjoy themselves and do what is good in
their lifetime....

— ECCLESIASTES 3:12

O Lord, my heart is not proud
    nor my look haughty;
    I do not aspire to great things

or to what is beyond me;
but I have taught myself to be contented
like a weaned child with its mother;
like a weaned child am I in my mind.

— PSALMS 131:1–2

Fashion a pure heart for me, O God;
create in me a steadfast spirit.

— PSALMS 51:12

AFTERWORD

The wisdom of Judaism is an ever-filling fountain of guidance and inspiration. It will never cease, and this volume would not be complete without the wisdom of some of those who have contributed to this vast body of knowledge in more recent times.

For thousands of years people have found Judaism a rich, artistic, and holy path of living. There is an enormous effort in our time to seek out ways to lengthen life. Here is a way to deepen it.... Inside each soul there are chambers, and chambers within chambers. Most of us open the door to a few compartments of our soul and leave the rest undisturbed. Judaism impels us to keep looking and, in the process, to discover that as we open these chambers to ourselves, we are more open to God as well.

— DAVID J. WOLPE, *Why Be Jewish?*

To be Jewish is to be a seeker of the unlimited ways in which God can be realized within our lives. A Hasidic saying urges us to hold on to two thoughts: that "the world was created for my sake" and that "I am but dust and ashes." When we feel small and insignificant, we must remember that we are created in God's image and that the world was created for our sake. When we are feeling powerful, we must recall our mortality. Our lives have purpose and ultimate significance as the manifestation of God in the world. . . .

We believe that God is the hidden ideal to which we always aspire through our daily routines, our religious practices, our learning, and our prayers. The higher world is the world to which we aspire, but it is also one that we can realize only within ourself, in our relationships, and in our community. Touching the transcendent reality greater than ourself is the spiritual goal of Judaism. The realization of our aspiration can only be achieved within the world we know.

— DAVID S. ARIEL,
*What Do Jews Believe?: The Spiritual
Foundations of Judaism*

Judaism, my child, is the struggle to bring down God upon earth, a struggle for sanctification of the human heart. This struggle your people wages not with physical force but with spirit and by constant striving for truth and justice. So, do you understand, my child, how we are distinct from others and wherein lies the secret of our existence on earth?

— A JEWISH MOTHER TO HER CHILD LIVING
IN THE WARSAW GHETTO, 1940, SHORTLY BEFORE
THEY WERE MURDERED BY THE NAZIS

Strange is our situation here upon earth.
Each of us comes for a short visit, not
    knowing why, yet sometimes seeming
to divine a purpose. From the standpoint
    of daily life, however, there is one thing we know:

That we are here for the sake of
others.... Above all, for those upon
    whose smile and well-being our
own happiness depends, and also for the
    countless unknown souls with whose fate
    we are connected by a bond of sympathy.

Many times a day I realize how much
my own outer and inner life is built upon

the labors of my fellow men, both living
and dead, and how earnestly I must
exert myself in order to give in return
as much as I have received.

— ALBERT EINSTEIN, "My Credo"

Human worth does not lie in riches or power, but in
character or goodness.... If people would only begin
to develop this goodness.... Give of yourself.... You
can always give something, even if it is only kindness.... No one has ever become poor from giving.

— ANNE FRANK, *The Diary of Anne Frank*

It was past midnight. I was walking through the
deserted city to my hotel on the other side of the river.
The night was dark and foggy and I couldn't get a
taxi. As I approached the bridge, I noticed a shabby
figure leaning over the parapet. A "down-and-out," I
thought. Then he disappeared. I heard a splash. My
God, I thought, he's done it. Suicide!

I ran back under the bridge, onto the embankment, and waded into the river, grabbing him as he
came past, borne by the current. I dragged him up
onto the embankment. He was quite a young guy. He
was still breathing. A couple of people noticed and I

shouted to them to get an ambulance. They managed to stop a taxi and between us we half dragged, half carried the man into the taxi.... I got in and told [the driver] to drive to the nearest hospital emergency room. I waited until the man was admitted, gave my report and got a taxi back to my hotel at last.

I had ruined a good suit and knew I would have a terrible cold in the morning. I could feel it coming on. But anyway I had saved a life. I had a hot bath and got into bed but it still worried me. Such a young man! Why had he done it?

The next morning, as soon as I was free, I bought a large bunch of grapes and set off for the hospital. I was determined to find out what was behind this matter. Maybe I could help.

Why was I so interested in the guy? In this great city there were at least half a dozen would-be suicides every night. Their plight did not touch me. Then it dawned on me. Of couse. First you *give*, then you *care*. I had given quite a lot. I had risked my life and gotten a bad cold in the bargain. I had invested something of myself in that man. Now my love and care were aroused. That's how it goes. First we *give*, then we come to love.

— Aryeh Carmell, *Masterplan: Judaism: Its Program, Meaning, Goals*

Imagine yourself in a situation where you are alone, wholly alone on earth, and you are offered one of the two, books or men. I often hear men prizing their solitude but that is only because there are still men somewhere on earth even though in the far distance. I knew nothing of books when I came forth from the womb of my mother, and I shall die without books, with another human hand in my own. I do, indeed, close my door at times and surrender myself to a book, but only because I can open the door again and see a human being looking at me.

— Martin Buber, *Meetings*

If you will always assume
the person sitting next to you is the messiah
waiting for some human kindness,

You will soon learn to weigh your words
and watch your hands.

And if he so chooses not to reveal himself
in your time,

It will not matter.

— Danny Siegel, transl., Proverb

One night I dreamed a dream. I was walking along the beach with my God. Across the sky flashed scenes from my life. For each scene, I noticed two sets of footprints in the sand, one belonging to me and the other belonging to God.

When the last scene of my life flashed before me, I looked back at the footprints in the sand. There was only one set of footprints. I realized that this was at the very lowest and saddest times of my life.

This really bothered me, so I questioned God.

"God, You told me when I decided to follow You that You would walk and be with me all the way. But I have noticed that during the most troublesome times of my life, there is only one set of footprints in the sand. I don't understand why, when I needed You the most, You would leave me."

And God said, "My precious child, I love you and will never leave you. During your times of trial and suffering, when you see only one set of footprints, *it was then that I carried you.*"

— MARGARET FISHBACK POWERS, "Footprints"

Judaism, done right, has the power to save your life from being spent entirely on the trivial.... But it can do more than that. Its goal is not just to make *your* life more satisfying. Its goal is not the survival of the

Jewish people. That is a means to an end, not an end in itself. The ultimate goal is to transform the world into the kind of world God had in mind when He created it.

— RABBI HAROLD KUSHNER,
To Life! A Celebration of Jewish Being and Thinking

Each of us has our special part, our special work to do, which we cannot shirk, even if we would, for it is forced upon us. To the most indifferent of us it must mean something for our good or ill, our weal or woe, that we are born Jews, into just these conditions in which we find ourselves, to work through them, if we can, into still higher conditions. We all stand at different points along the line, with some above us, some below, to help and to be helped. Judaism is to each of us a personal factor, an individual problem, as well as a large race-question, to be solved individually as well as collectively, — a problem as old as the world, which will be older yet before it is solved. But if we see any light, we need not despair. We can believe, we can hope and trust, and above all, we can serve. "For now abideth faith, hope, and love, these three; but the greatest of these is love."

— JOSEPHINE LAZARUS, *The Spirit of Judaism*

One of the most important goals which you can set

yourself to achieve is the realization of God's presence in your life. I deem it so important because if you can attain to this realization, you will be lifted above all the cares and anxieties of life, you will find that life no longer has the power to hurt you, you will find that life assumes wonderful meaning and joy, you will find yourself safe and secure even in the midst of the greatest vicissitudes and storms, you will find a way out of your difficulties, you will find an assured way to happiness, an assured way to inner peace and serenity, a staff against the pitfalls and roughness of the road, a shelter against the four winds of heaven, a refuge from the storm of adverse circumstances, a shield and a buckler against your enemies, a rock to lean upon when your feet are weary, a mountain top to be lifted to when the tide of adversity is rising about you. All this, and more, much more than my poor pen can convey, will be yours when you truly realize that God is there, that He is beside you, that His love is about you, and His care is watching over you, and His strength is available to you. If the knowledge of the presence of God means all this, surely you must want to attain to this knowledge, to this awareness of God's presence.

— TEHILLA LICHTENSTEIN,
"God in the Silence," *Jewish Science Interpreter*
(Danny Siegel, transl.)

Nothing in life just happens. You have to have the stamina to meet obstacles and overcome them. To struggle.... Don't become cynical. Don't give up hope.... There is idealism in this world. There is human brotherhood.

— GOLDA MEIR (1898-1978)

One final old Jewish legend:

Just like God, every eternal soul has all knowledge of the universe. Yet when a soul comes to earth and is placed in a physical body, it cannot bring with it the totality of knowledge; for on earth the soul must be delimited by the boundaries of human existence.

Just before a soul, now in the body of a baby in the womb, emerges into human life, an angel taps the baby on the upper lip — creating that little indentation right under the nose — and in so doing takes away the entirety of knowledge.

The soul, now a human being, lives its earthborn existence. But no matter how pleasing and satisfying its human sojourn, the soul — at its deepest and most hidden place — always feels a tinge of emptiness, a tinge of sadness. For at the core of its being, the soul sees tiny glimpses of all it once knew, and it sees momentary flashes of what it can know — and be — again.

That is why the soul-voyage of earthly existence is, at the same time, a journey back to the source, back to ultimate origin, back to infinite knowledge, back to God.

The angel — who feels bad for having taken away soul-knowledge — becomes a life guide.

And God — to whom each and every soul is a precious, eternal partner — gently shows the soul the way back to what it once had and what it will have again.

On earth — as they are through eternity — God's directions for the journey, the pathways back to all knowledge, are in the life-gift of Torah. Torah, and the Jewish teachings, traditions, and faith community that come from it, is the earthly bridge to the soul-world of spirit.

— RABBI WAYNE DOSICK,
Living Judaism: The Complete Guide to
Jewish Belief, Tradition and Practice

ABOUT THE EDITOR

ACKNOWLEDGMENTS

ACKNOWLEDGMENTS

DALE SALWAK, a professor of English at Southern California's Citrus College, has taught courses and conducted seminars on biblical history and literature for over twenty-five years. He was educated at Purdue University and then the University of Southern California under a National Defense Education Act competitive fellowship program. In 1985 he was awarded a National Endowment for the Humanities grant. In 1987 Purdue University awarded him its Distinguished Alumni Award. He is widely published; his works include seventeen books on various contemporary literary figures as well as *The Words of Christ* and *The Wonders of Solitude* (both New World Library).

ABOUT RABBI YECHIEL ECKSTEIN

Rabbi, author, lecturer, radio and television host, YECHIEL ECKSTEIN is the Founder and President of the International Fellowship of Christians and Jews. He is the author of five highly acclaimed books: *How Firm a Foundation; What You Should Know About Jews and Judaism; Understanding Evangelicals: A Guide for the Jewish Community; Ask the Rabbi;* and *Five Questions Most Frequently Asked About Jews and Judaism.* Yechiel Eckstein was ordained as a rabbi at Yeshiva University in New York City and completed the studies for his doctorate at Columbia University. He serves on the national Board of Directors of the American Refugee Committee.

For their generous help with this project I am indebted especially to the following good people: Robert Baxt, Dr. Reginald Clarke, Rabbi Yechiel Eckstein, Dr. Aubrey Fine, Laura Nagy, Dr. Lloyd J. Ogilvie, my parents Dr. Stanley and Frances H. Salwak, James Shuemaker, and my wife Patti.

BIBLIOGRAPHY

Ariel, David S. *What Do Jews Believe? The Spiritual Foundations of Judaism*. NY: Shocken Books, 1995.

Baron, Joseph L., ed. *A Treasury of Jewish Quotations*. Northvale, NJ: Jason Aronson, 1985.

Birnbaum, Philip, ed. *The Encyclopedia of Jewish Concepts*. Rockaway Beach, NY: Hebrew Publishing Co., 1964.

Bokser, Ben Zion, trans. *The Prayer Book: Weekday, Sabbath and Festival*. Rockaway Beach, NY: Hebrew Publishing Co., 1957.

Braude, William G., trans. *The Midrash on Psalms*. 2 vols. New Haven: Yale University Press, 1959.

————., trans. *Peskita Rabbati*. Vol. 1. New Haven: Yale University Press, 1968.

Buber, Martin. *Meetings*. Ed. Maurice Friedman. La Salle, IL: Open Court, 1973.

Carmell, Aryeh. *Masterplan: Judaism: Its Program, Meaning, Goals*. Jerusalem: Jerusalem Academy Publications, 1991.

Cohen, A., ed. *Everyman's Talmud*. NY: E.P. Dutton, 1949.

————. *The Minor Tractates of the Talmud*. 2 vols., 2d ed. NY: Soncino Press, 1971.

Danby, Herbert, trans. *The Mishnah*. London: Oxford University Press, 1933.

Dosick, Rabbi Wayne. *Living Judaism: The Complete Guide to Jewish Belief, Tradition and Practice*. NY: HarperCollins, 1995.

Epstein, I., trans. *The Babylonian Talmud*. NY: Soncino Press, 1948.

Feinsilver, Alexander, trans. *The Talmud for Today*. NY: St. Martin's Press, 1980.

Frank, Anne. *The Diary of Anne Frank*. Garden City, NY: Doubleday, 1952.

Freedman, H. and Maurice Simon, trans. *Midrash Rabbah*. NY: Soncino Press, 1983.

Glatzer, Nahum N., ed. *Hammer on the Rock: A Short Midrash Reader*. NY: Schocken Books, 1948.

Goldin, Judah, trans. *The Living Talmud: The Wisdom of the Fathers*. NY: New American Library, 1957.

Goodman, Philip, ed. *The Rosh Hashanah Anthology*. Philadelphia: Jewish Publication Society of America, 1973.

Hebrew-English Edition of the Babylonian Talmud. NY: Traditional Press, 1982.

Heinemann, Joseph. *Prayer in the Talmud: Forms and Patterns*. NY: De Gruyter, 1977.

Herford, R. Travers, ed. *The Ethics of the Talmud: Sayings of the Fathers*. NY: Schocken Books, 1925, 1962.

Hertz, Joseph J., ed. *Sayings of the Fathers*. NY: Behrman House, 1945.

Kahane, Rabbi Chas., ed. *Torah Yesharah: A Traditional Interpretive Translation of the Five Books of Moses*. NY: Torah Yesharah Publications, 1963.

Kushner, Harold. *To Life! A Celebration of Jewish Being and Thinking*. Boston: Little, Brown, 1993.

Montefiore, C.G. and H. Loewe, eds. *A Rabbinic Anthology*. NY: Schocken Books, 1974.

Moore, George Foote. *Judaism in the First Centuries of the Christian Era*. Vol. 1. Cambridge: Harvard University Press, 1927.

Newman, Louis I. and Samuel Spitz, eds. *The Talmudic Anthology*. NY: Behrman House, 1945.

Petuchowski, Jacob J. *Our Masters Taught: Rabbinic Stories and Sayings*. NY: Crossroad, 1982.

Scholem, Gershom, ed. *Zohar: The Book of Splendor*. NY: Schocken Books, 1949.

Siegel, Danny. *Where Heaven and Earth Touch: An Anthology of Midrash and Halachah*. Northvale, NJ: Jason Aronson, 1989.

Sperling, Harry and Maurice Simon, trans. *The Zohar*. NY: Soncino Press, 1934.

Telushkin, Rabbi Joseph. *Jewish Wisdom: Ethical, Spiritual, and Historical Lessons from the Great Works and Thinkers*. NY: William Morrow and Co., Inc., 1994.

Wolpe, David J. *Why Be Jewish?* NY: Henry Holt, 1995.

Also by Dale Salwak
and available from New World Library

The Words of Christ. This remarkable book distilled from the New Revised Standard Version contains the fundamental teachings of Christ arranged thematically to open up our understanding of familiar passages and to invite us to look more deeply within ourselves. A powerful reminder of where our traditions came from and of the great promises in store for us if we read and heed these words.

The Wonders of Solitude. More than 300 quotes that sparkle with meaning for the contemporary reader. A book everyone in our busy, noisy world can benefit from. Truly inspiring.

> *This book is a treasure chest of wisdom about how to enjoy time alone....I highly recommend this book for those who want to live life to the fullest.*
> —Lloyd John Ogilvie

> *Find a private, quiet place and indulge in this book.*
> —NAPRA Review